Fairy and Fantasy
Grayscale Coloring Book
by Christine Karron

FAIRY and FANTASY
Grayscale Coloring book by Christine Karron

First published July 2020

Copyright 2020 Christine Karron
All rights reserved

Other than for personal use or book review, no part of this book may be reproduced or transmitted in any form or by any means, electronic or mechanical, recording or by any information storage and retrieval system, without written permission from the copyright holder.

ISBN: 9798668509614
Imprint: Independently published

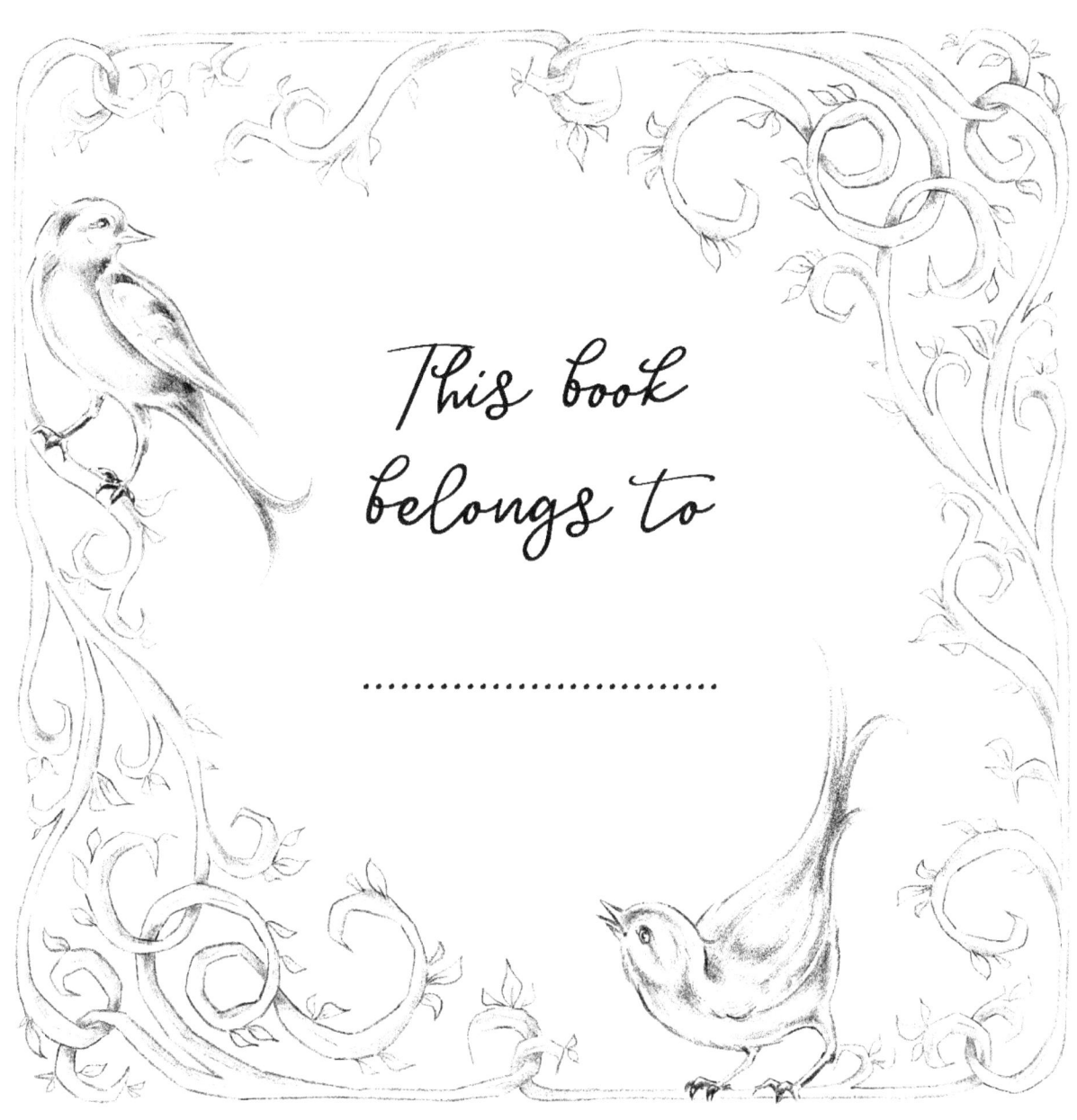

This book belongs to

....

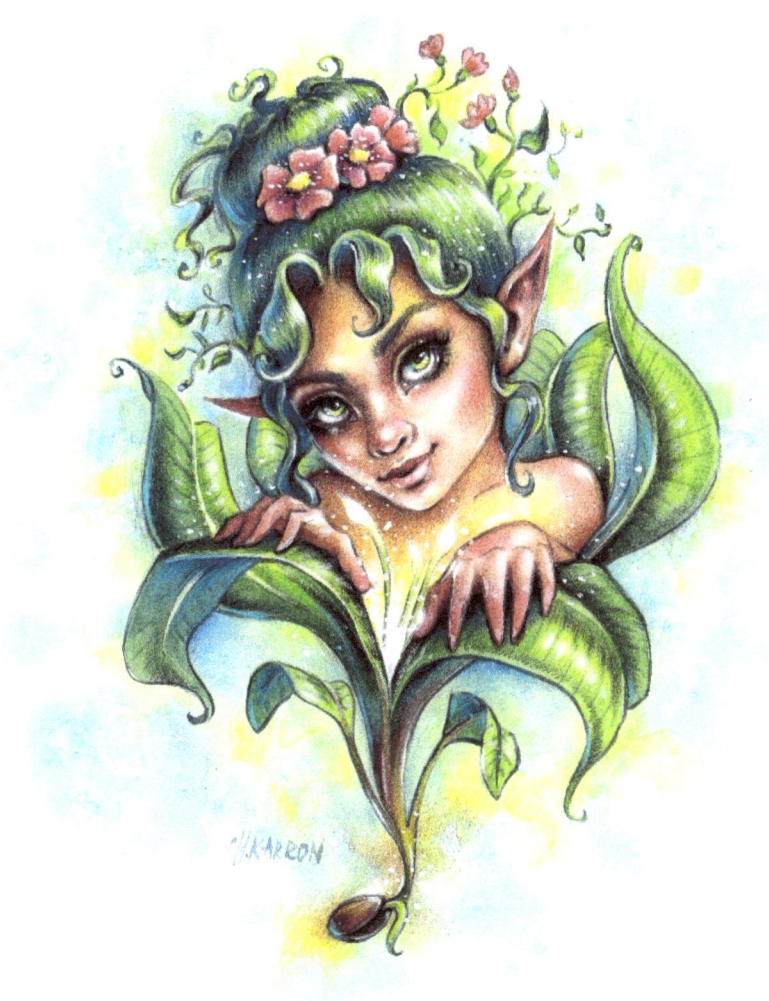

This coloring book is designed for experienced colorists and beginners as well. Recommended for coloring with markers, colored pencils, pens and/or crayons. If using wet media, place a sheet of thick paper or card stock behind the coloring page to prevent bleed through.

All illustrations in this book were originally created and traditionally hand drawn by the artist Christine Karron. For coloring inspirations, demo videos and more about Christine's artwork visit www.chkarron.com

Fairy and Fantasy

1. Fairy Ring
2. Wind Whispers
3. Grace Fairy
4. Whimsy Fairy Celise
5. Fae Messenger
6. Fox Rider
7. Forest Sprite
8. Fairy Magic
9. Raven Guide
10. Water Nymph
11. Unicorn Princess
12. Baby Dragon
13. Mr. Vampire
14. Tides of Time
15. Odette Swan Princess
16. Cowgirl Mermaid
17. Troll Girl
18. Fairytale Forest
19. Cookie Elves
20. Seedling

Bonus

21. Lilies and Pearls
22. Dear Diary
23. Kitty Cuddles
24. Bedtime Story

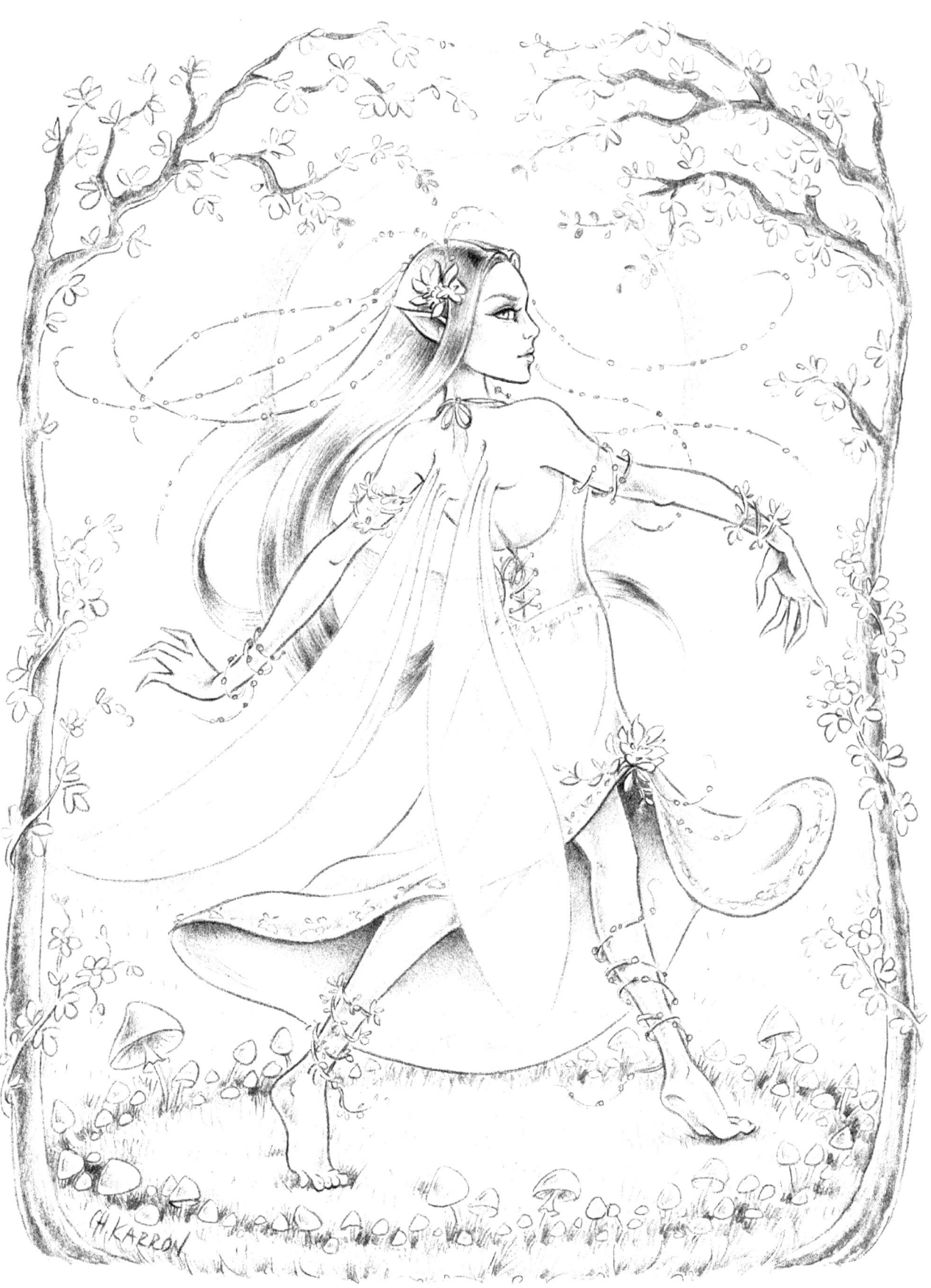

Fairy and Fantasy (c) Christine Karron — Fairy Ring

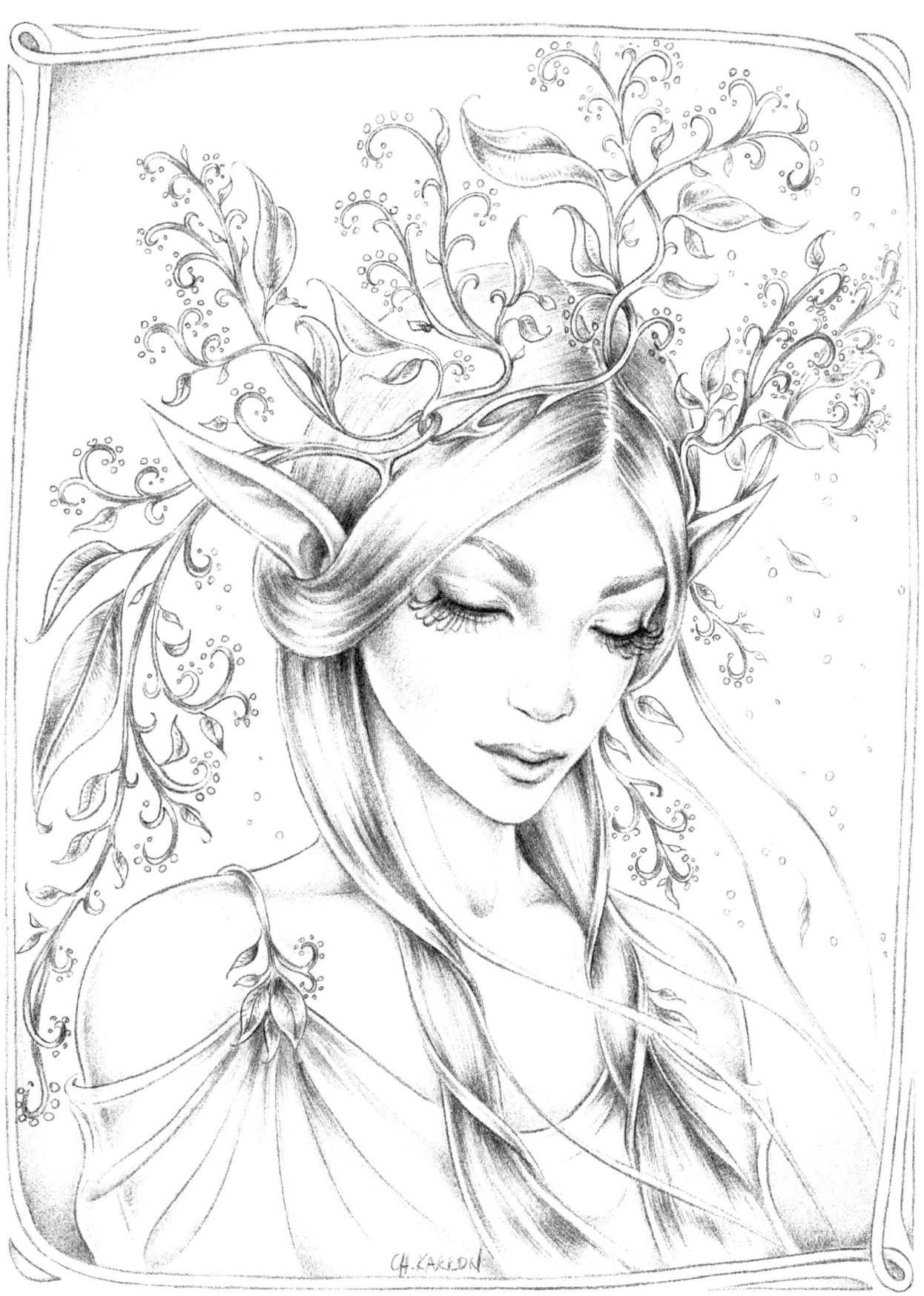

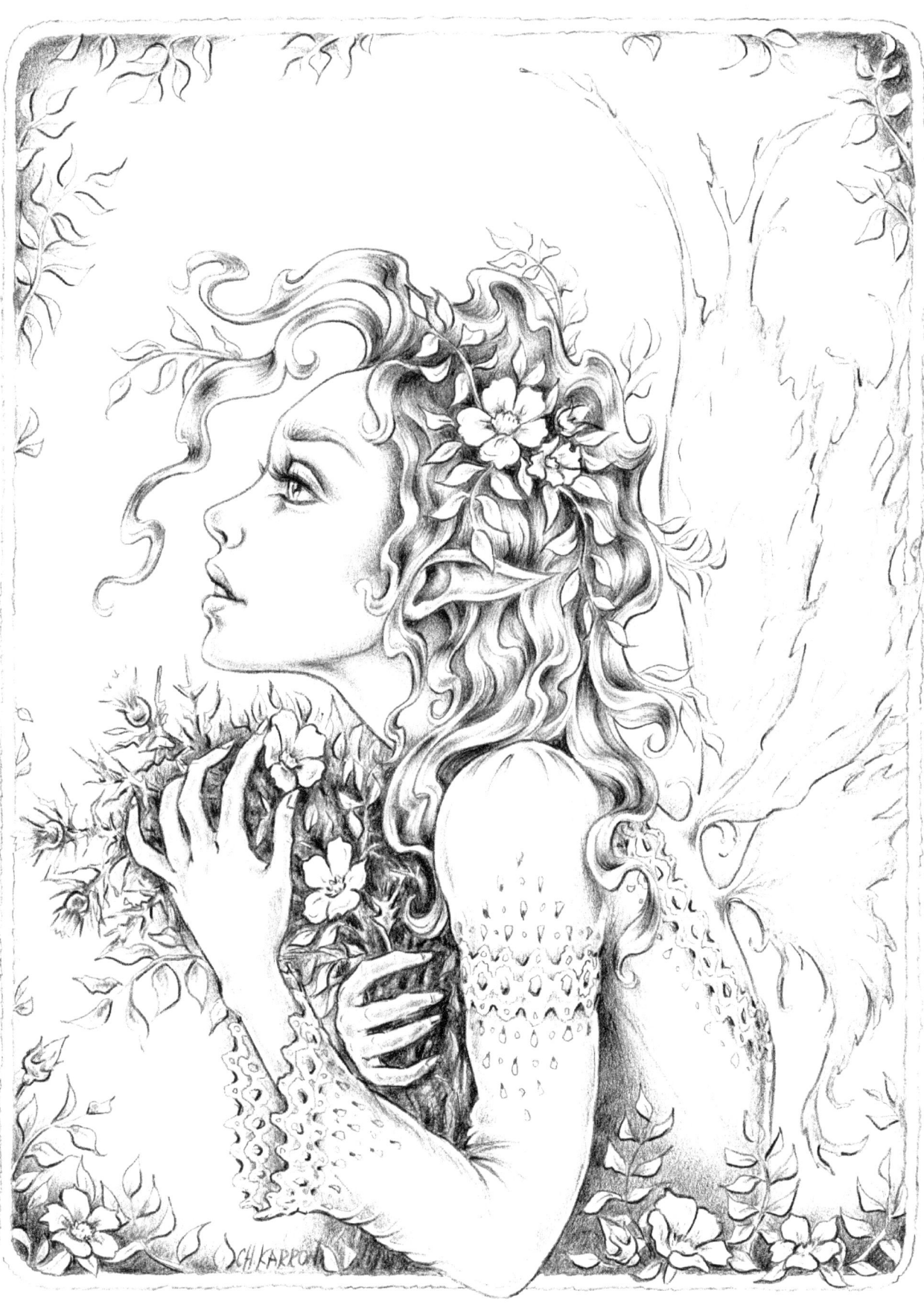

Fairy and Fantasy (c) Christine Karron   Grace Fairy

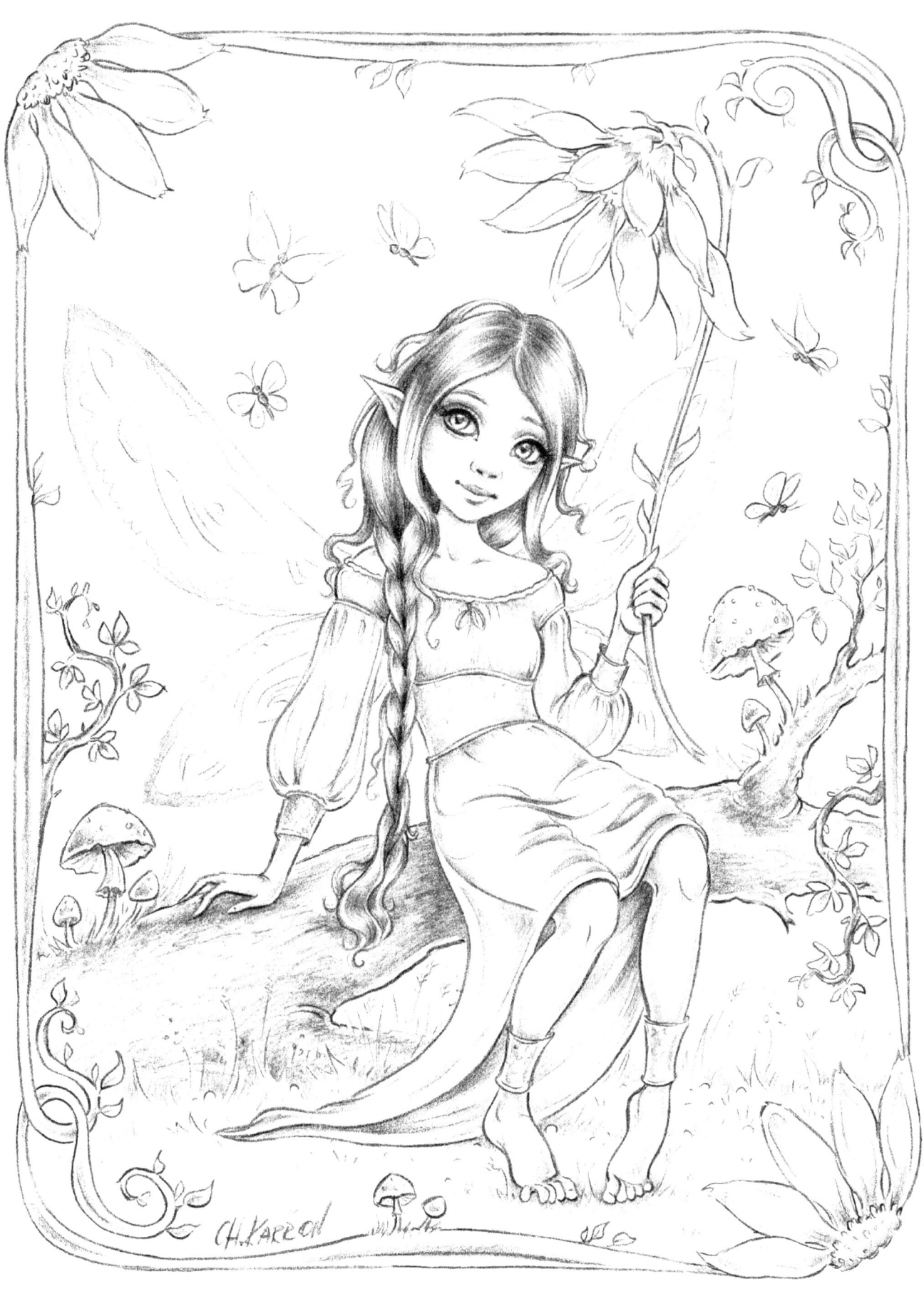

Fairy and Fantasy (c) Christine Karron

Whimsy Fairy Celise

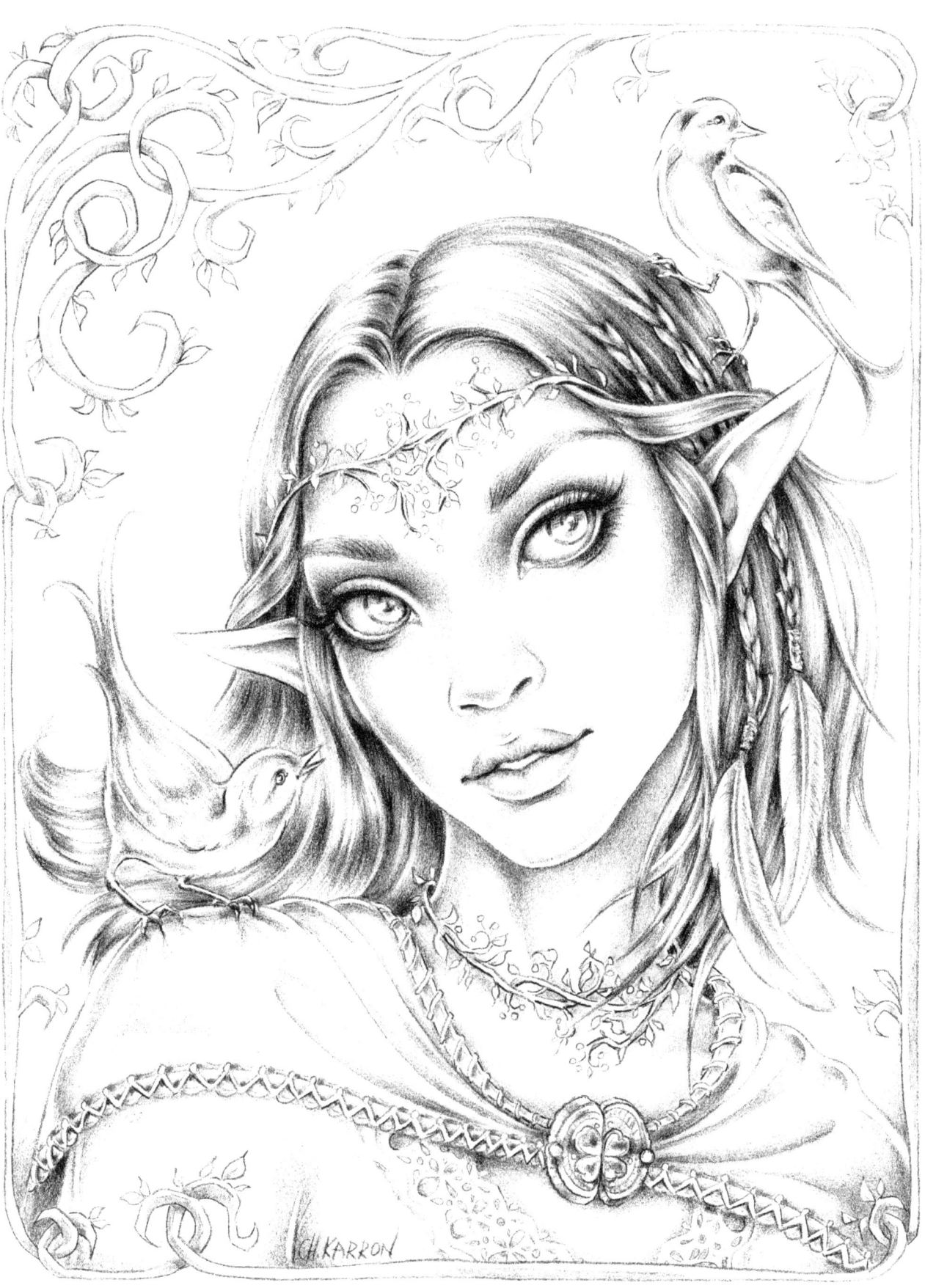

Fairy and Fantasy (c) Christine Karron

Fae Messengers

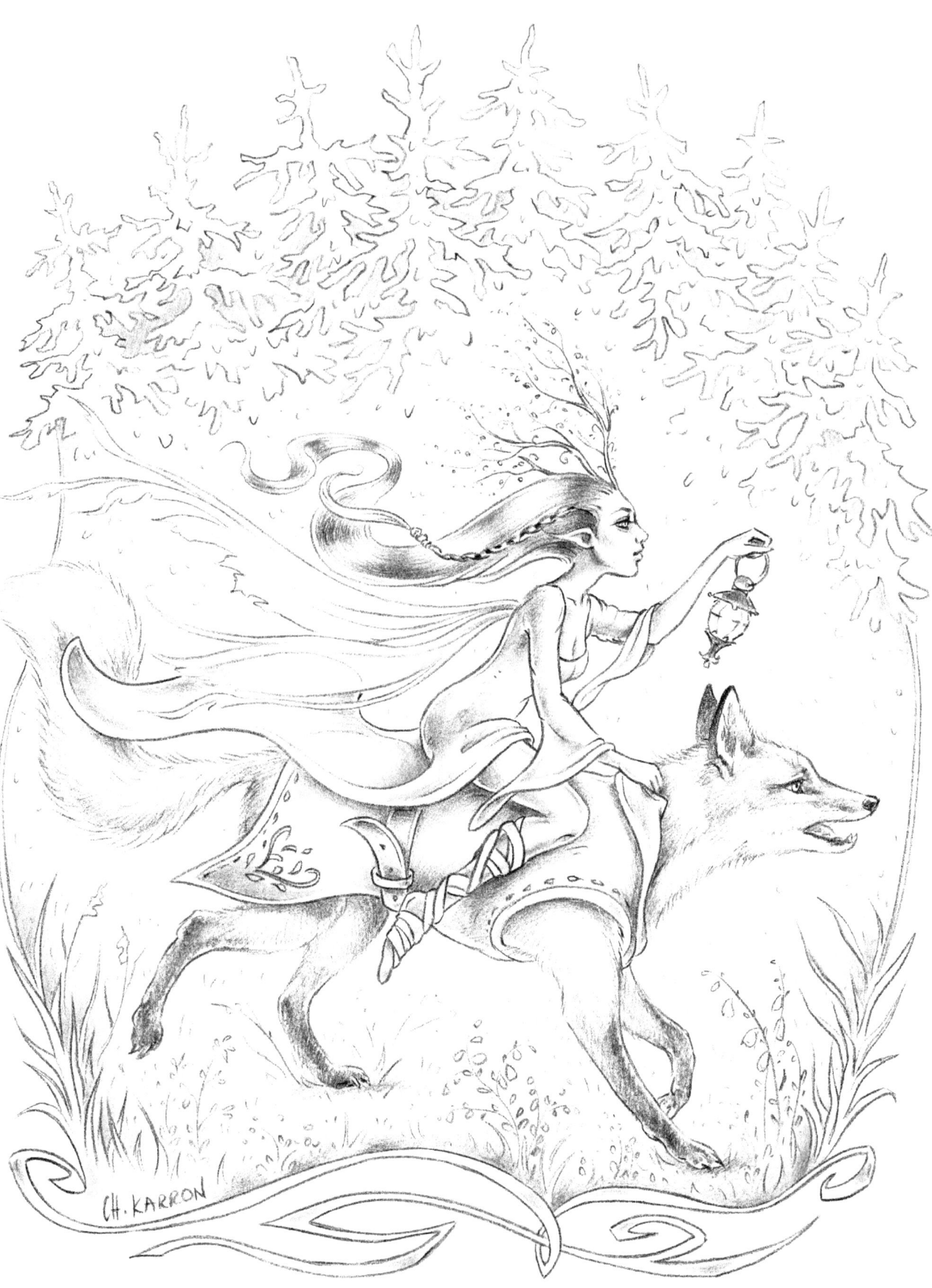

Fairy and Fantasy (c) Christine Karron — Fox Rider

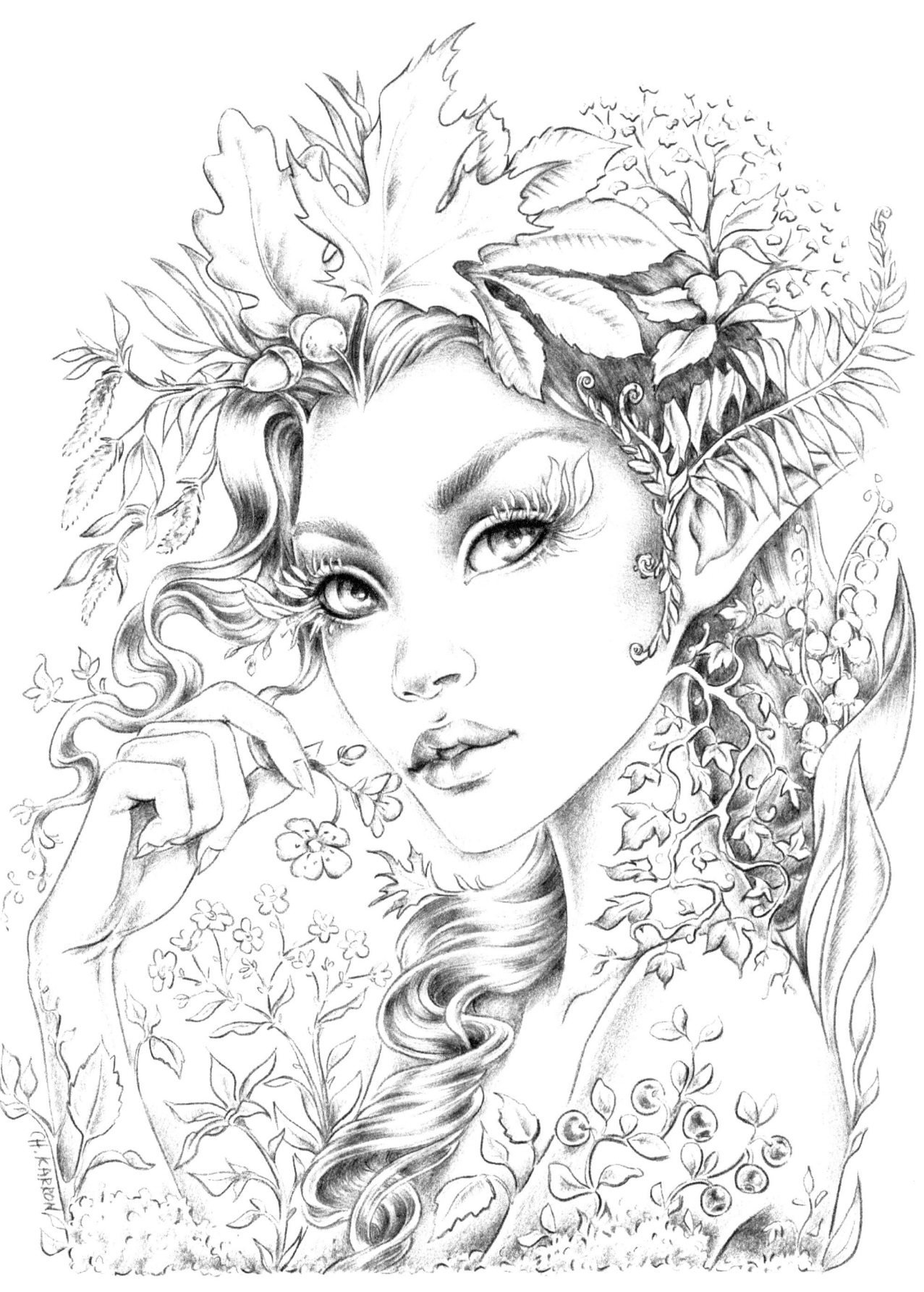

Fairy and Fantasy (c) Christine Karron — Forest Sprite

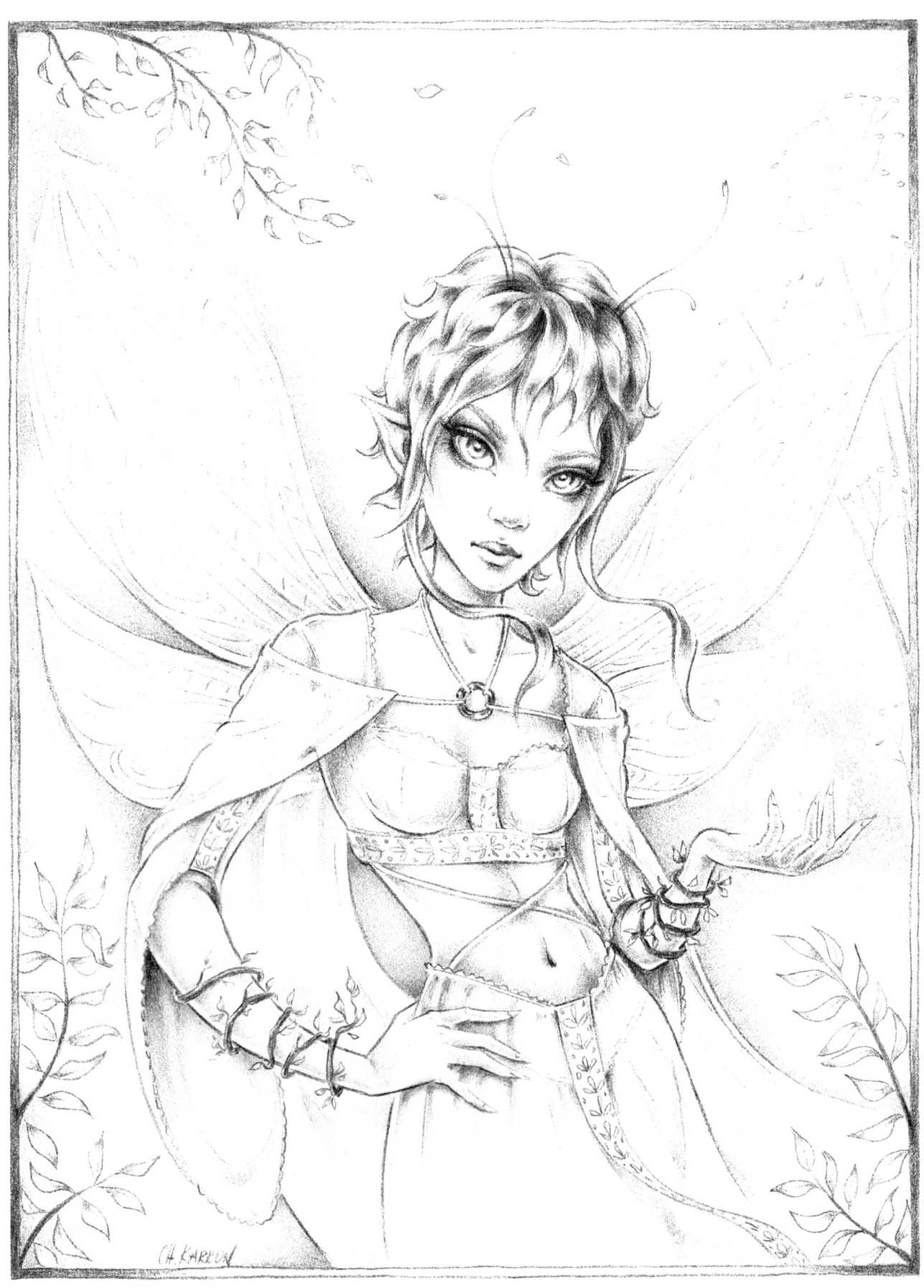

Fairy and Fantasy (c) Christine Karron — Fairy Magic

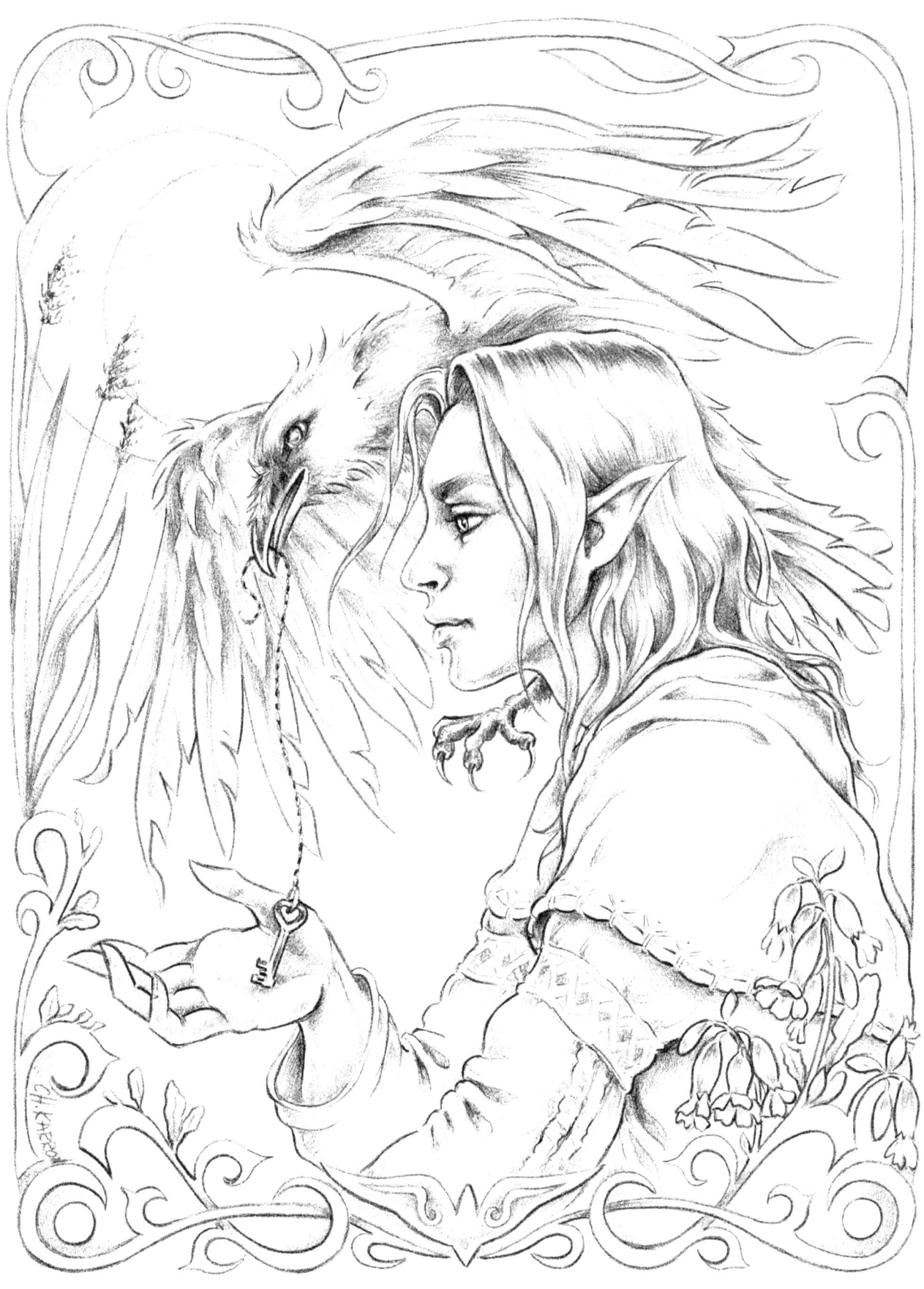

Fairy and Fantasy (c) Christine Karron — Raven Guide

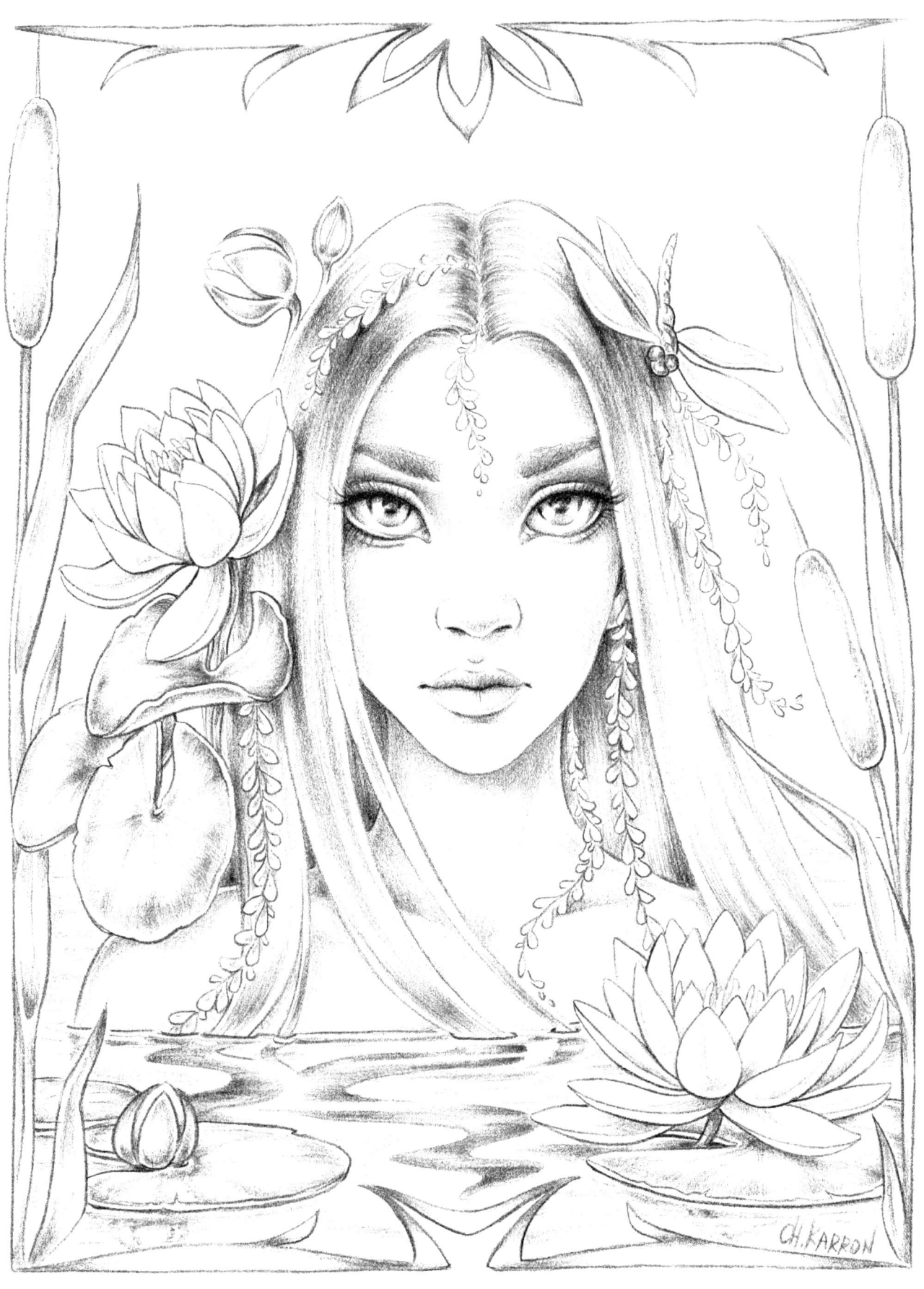

Fairy and Fantasy (c) Christine Karron

Water Nymph

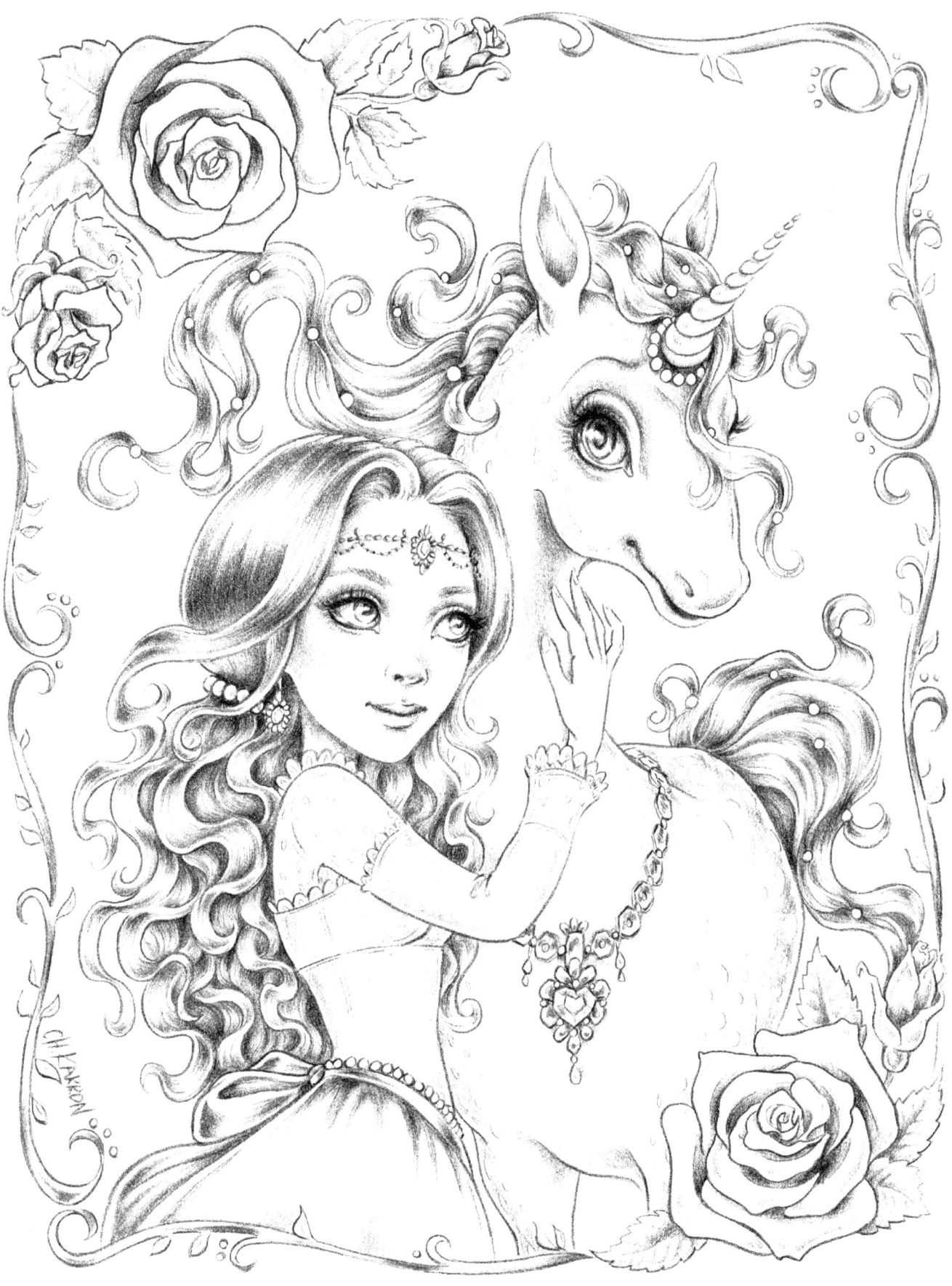

Fairy and Fantasy (c) Christine Karron — Unicorn Princess

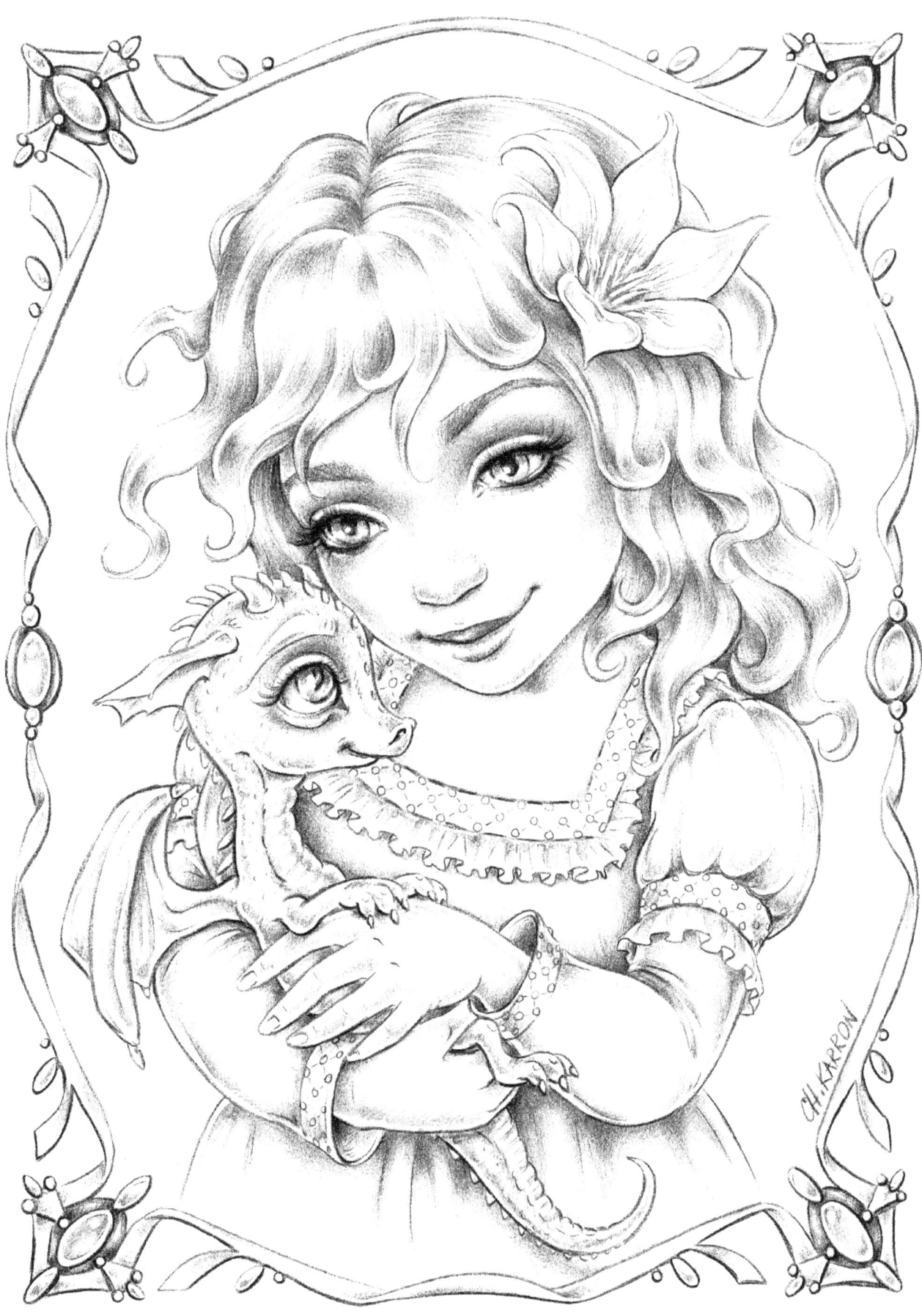
Fairy and Fantasy (c) Christine Karron   Baby Dragon

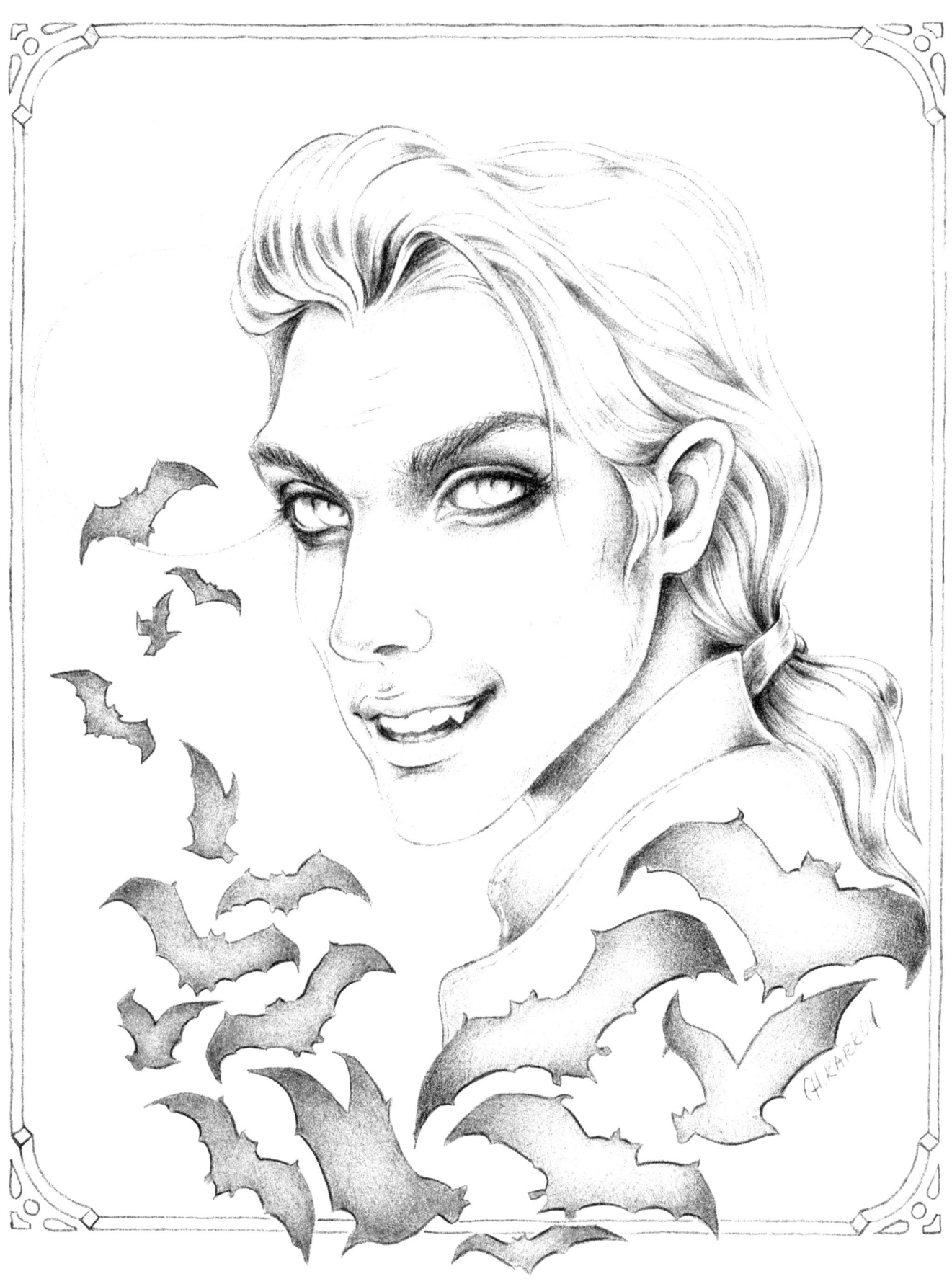

Fairy and Fantasy (c) Christine Karron — Mr. Vampire

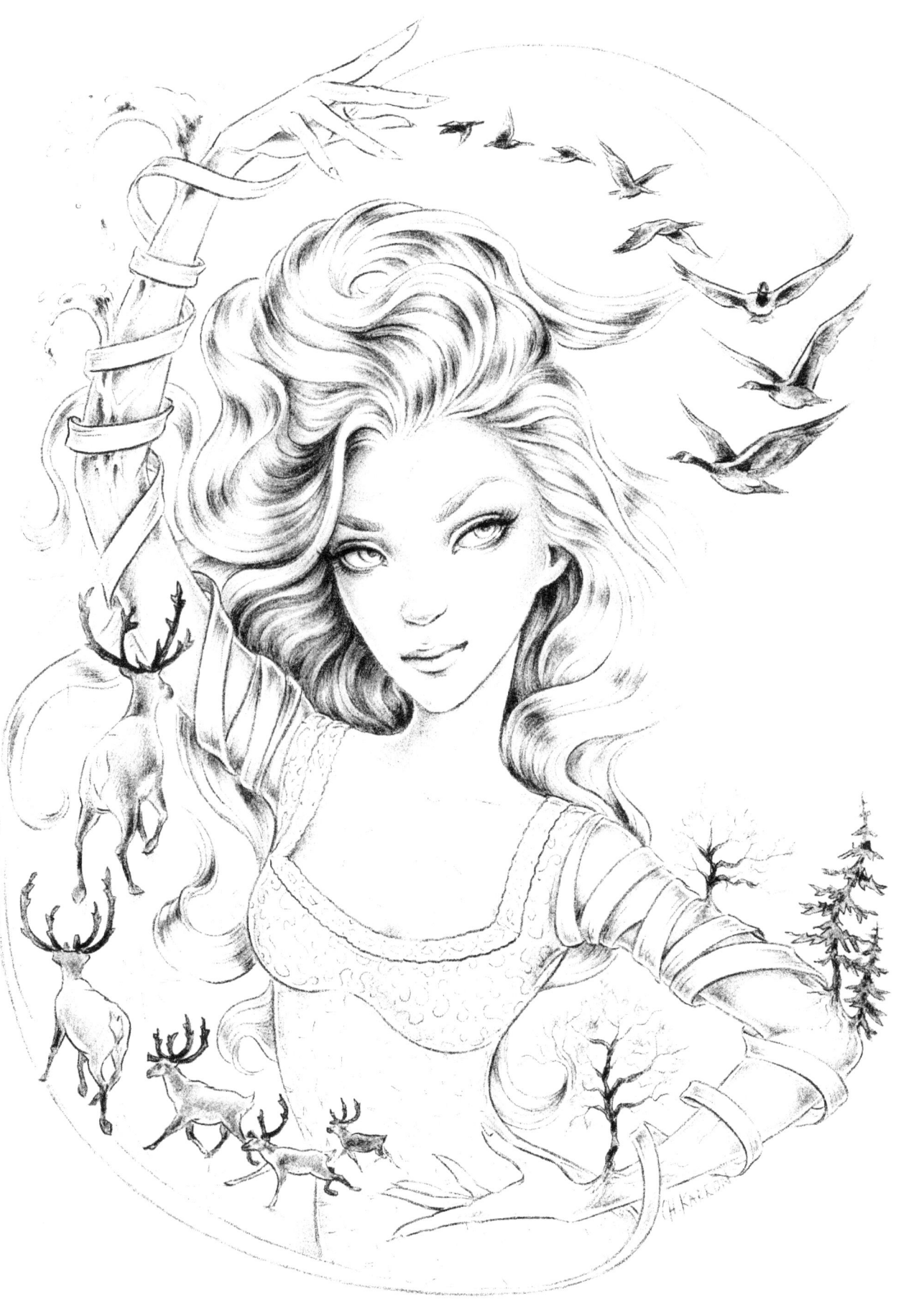

Fairy and Fantasy (c) Christine Karron — Tides of Time

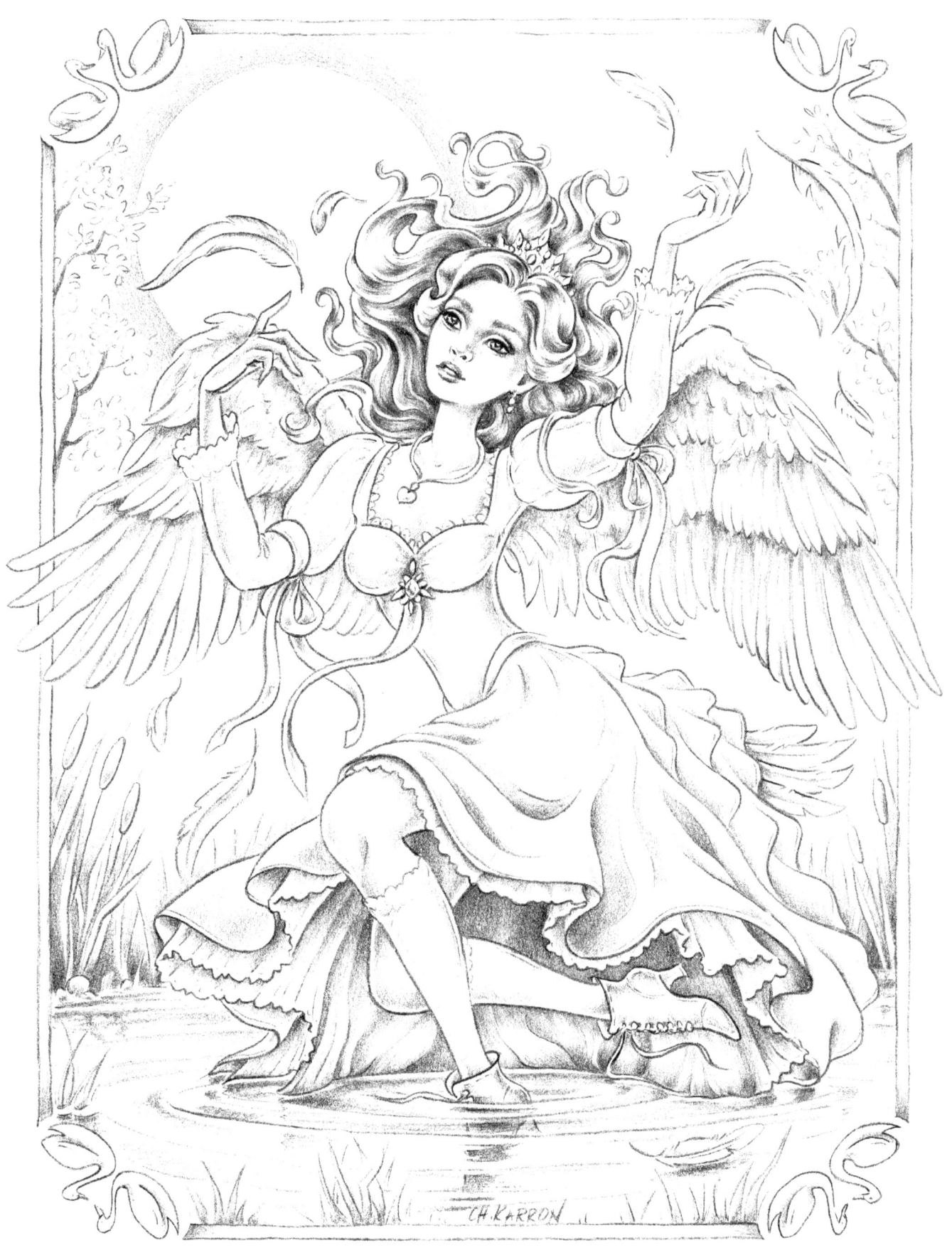

Fairy and Fantasy (c) Christine Karron Odette

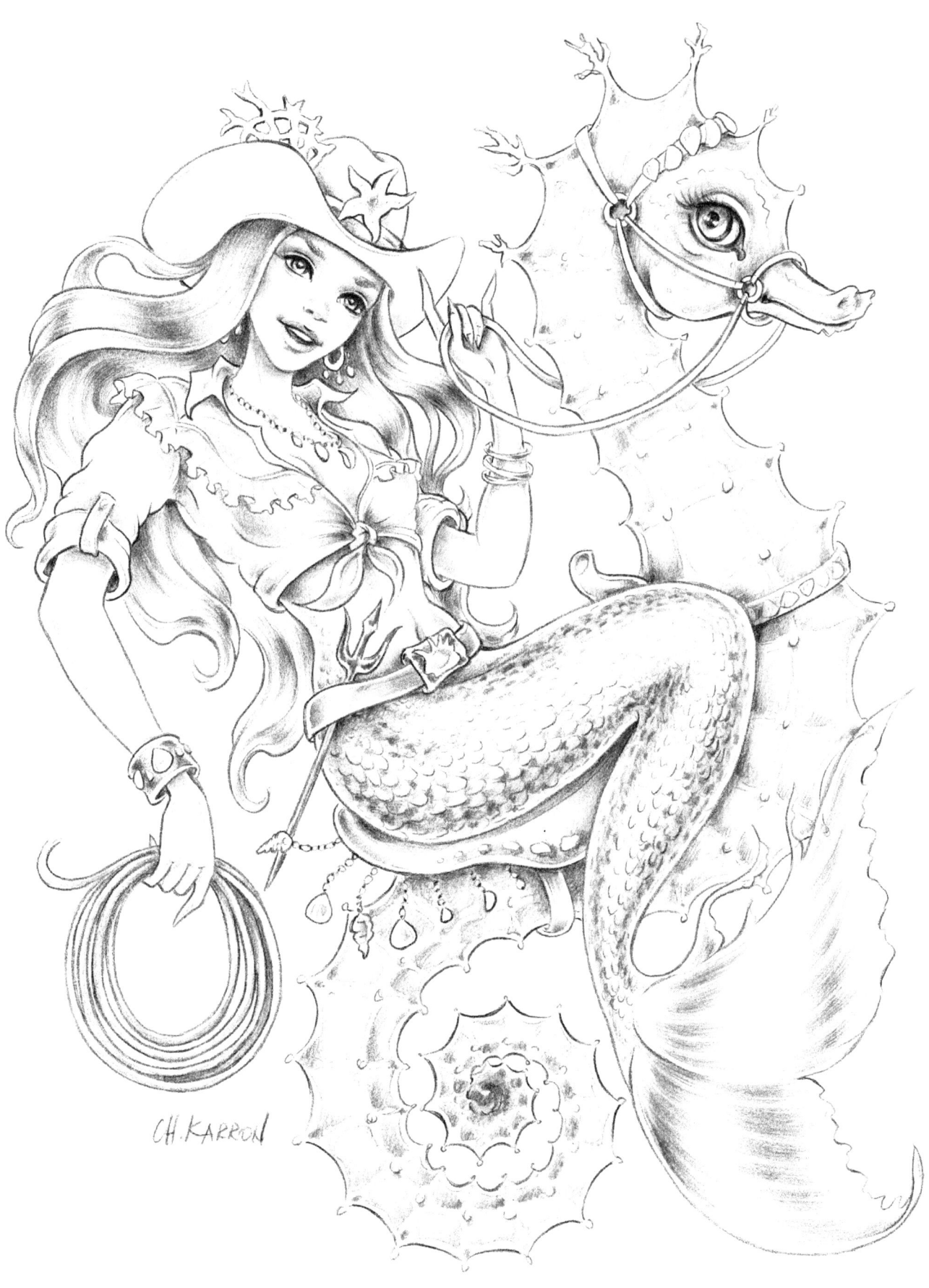

Fairy and Fantasy (c) Christine Karron — Cowgirl Mermaid

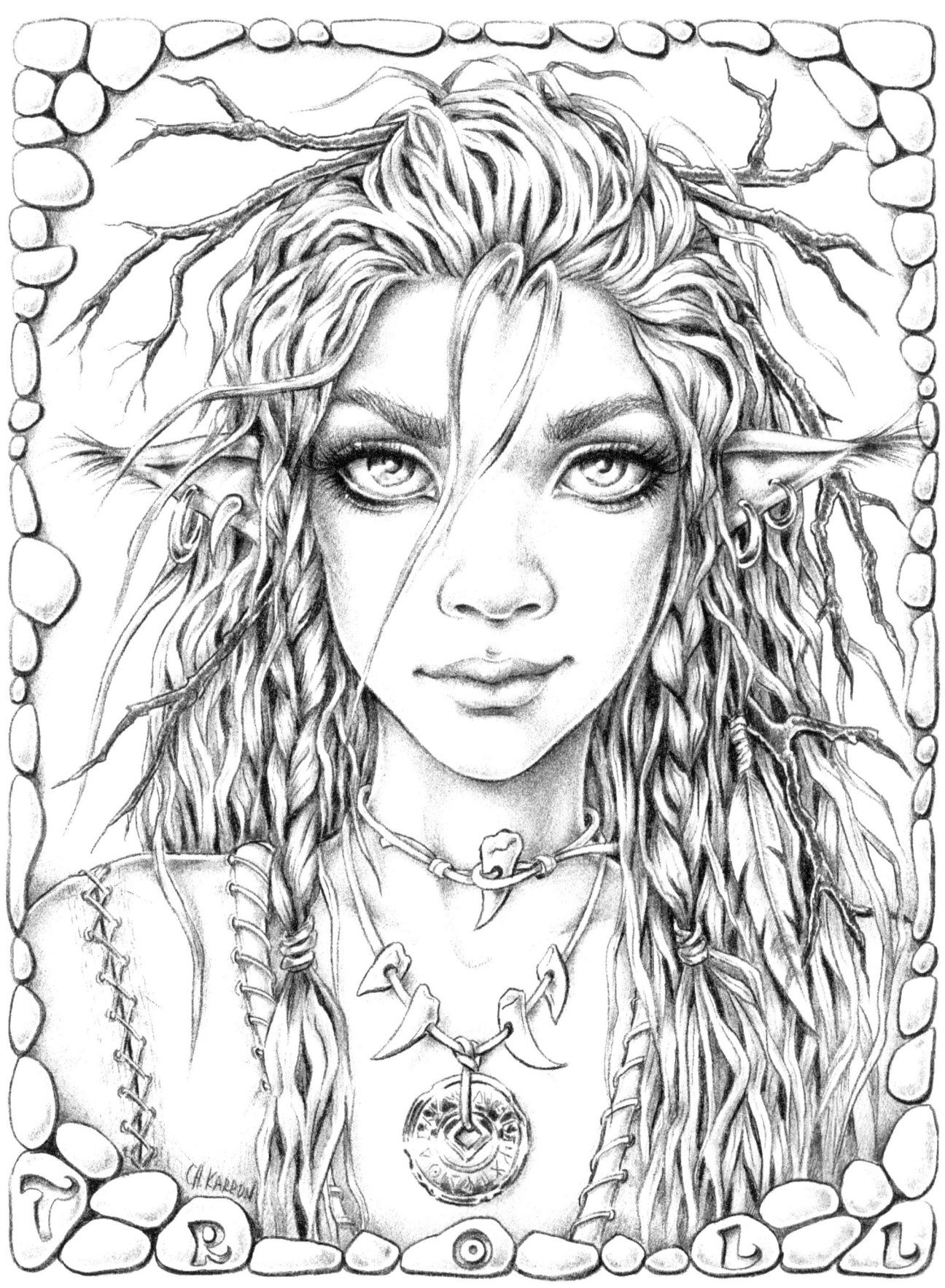

Fairy and Fantasy (c) Christine Karron — Troll Girl

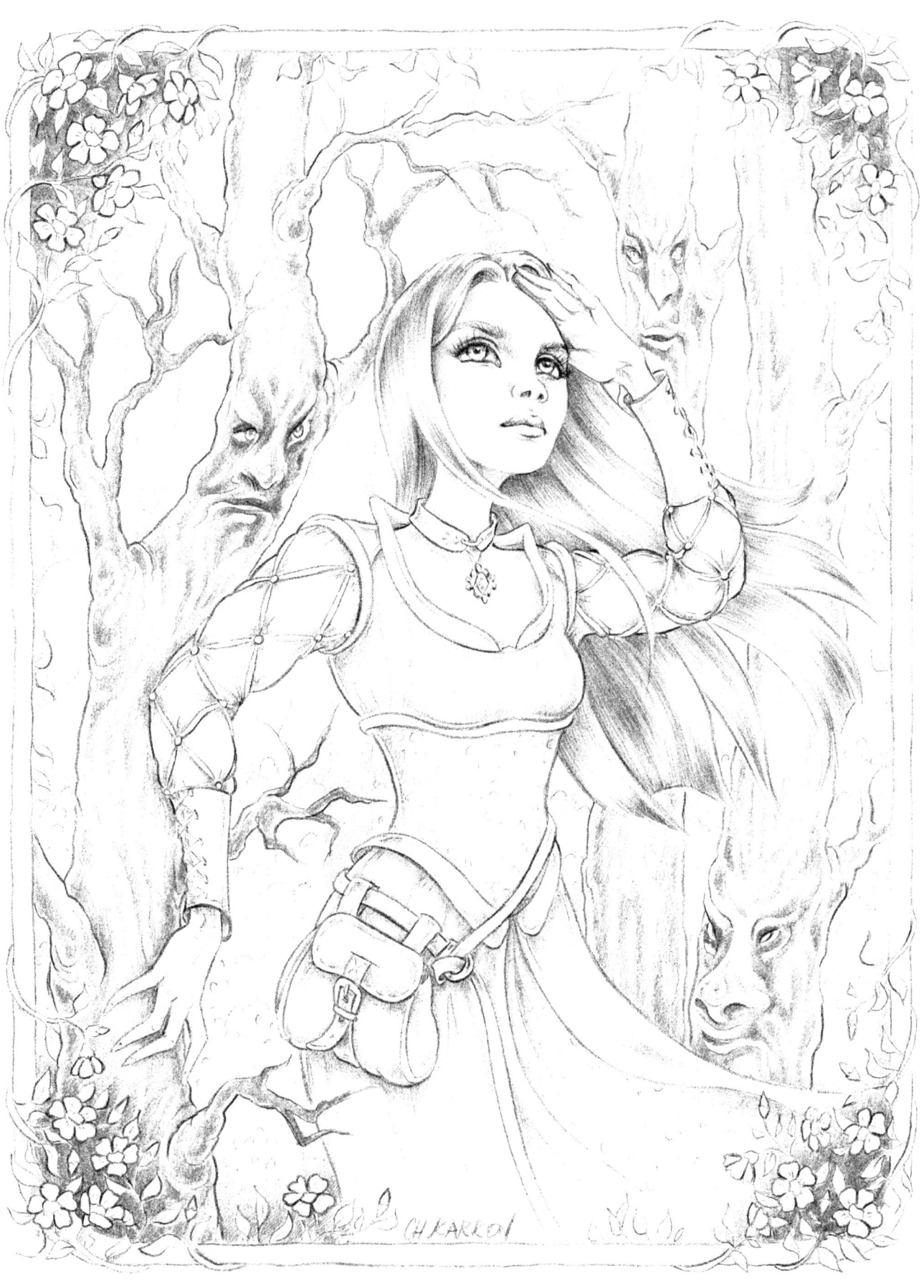

Fairy and Fantasy (c) Christine Karron — Fairytale Forest

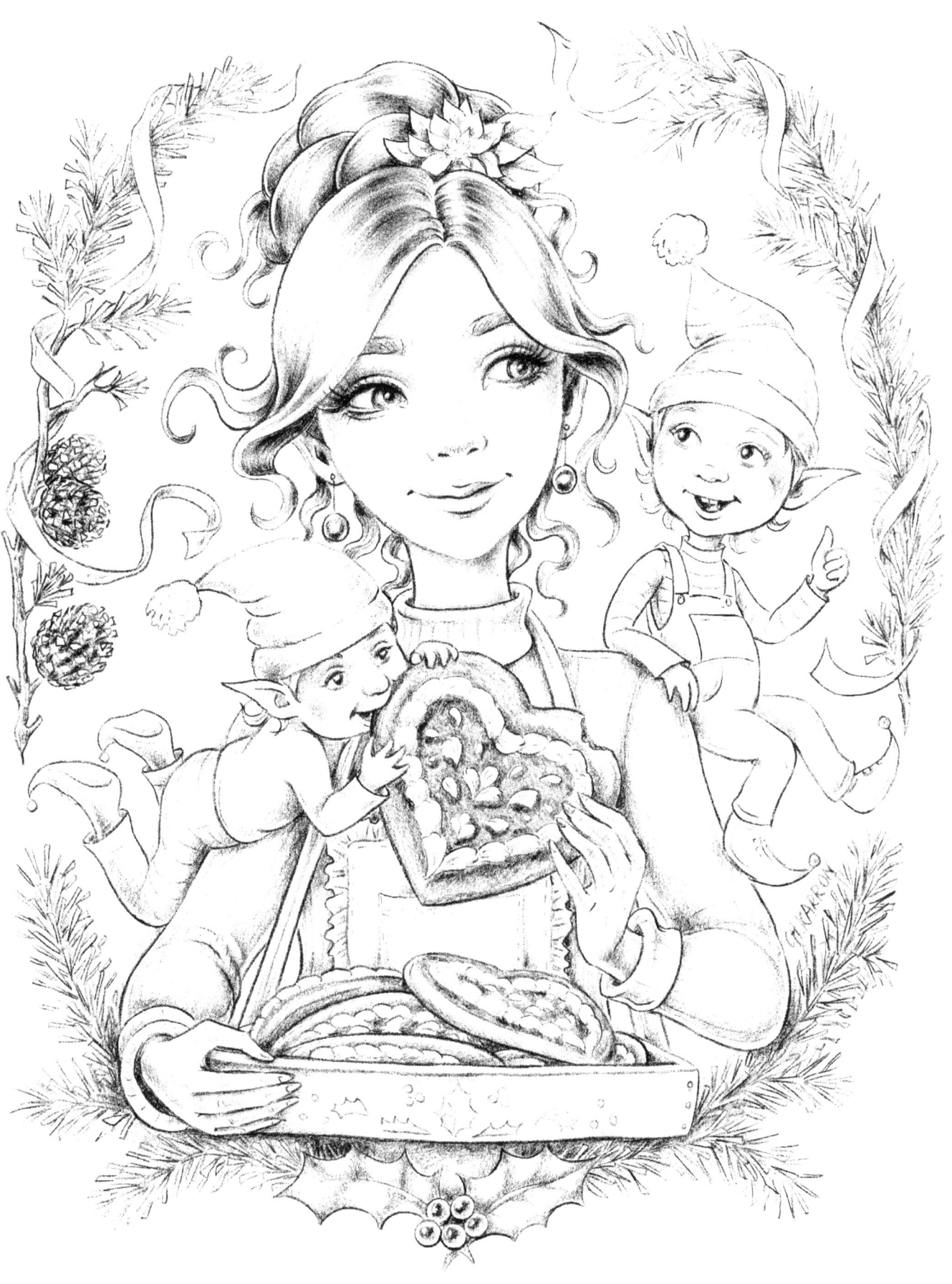

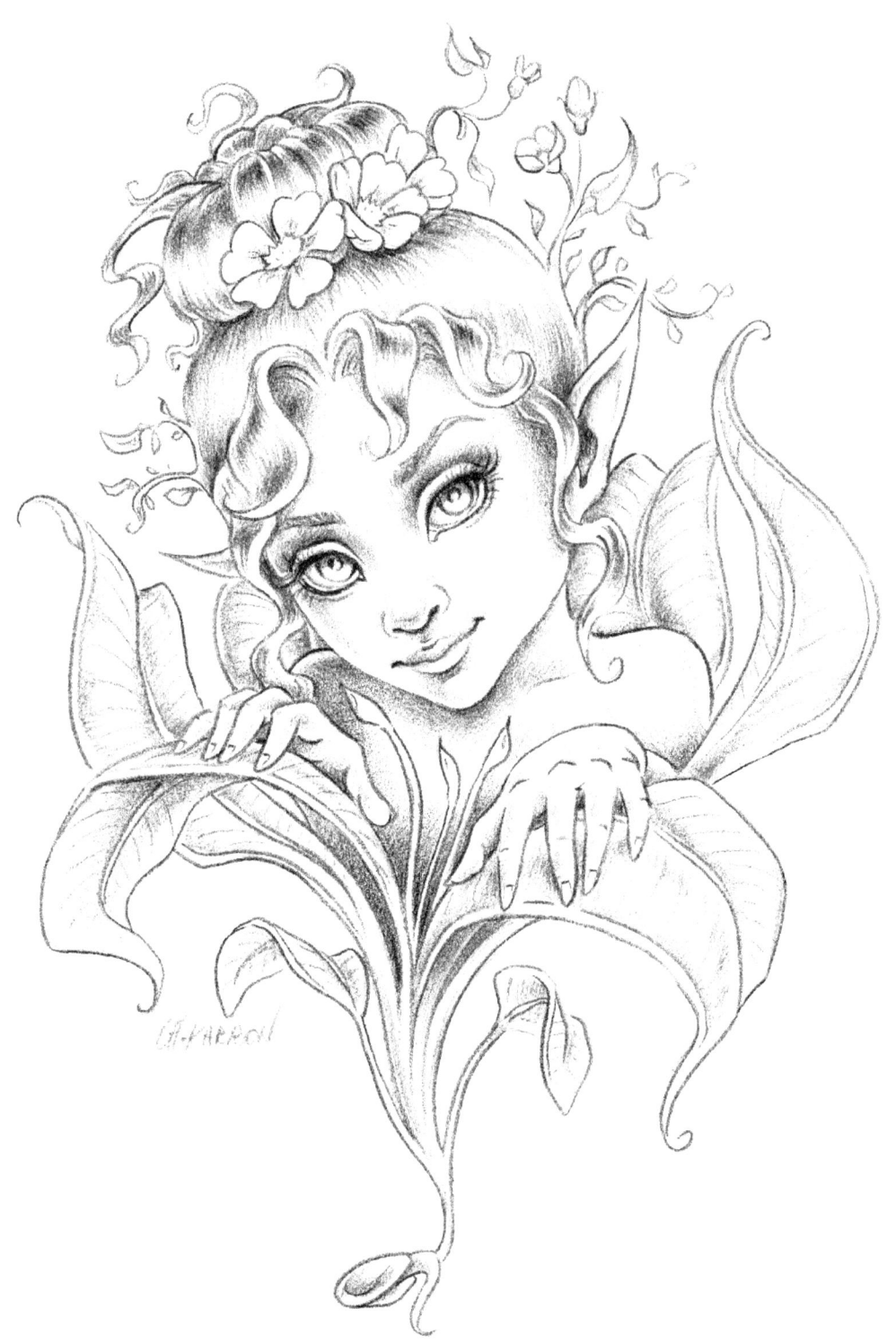

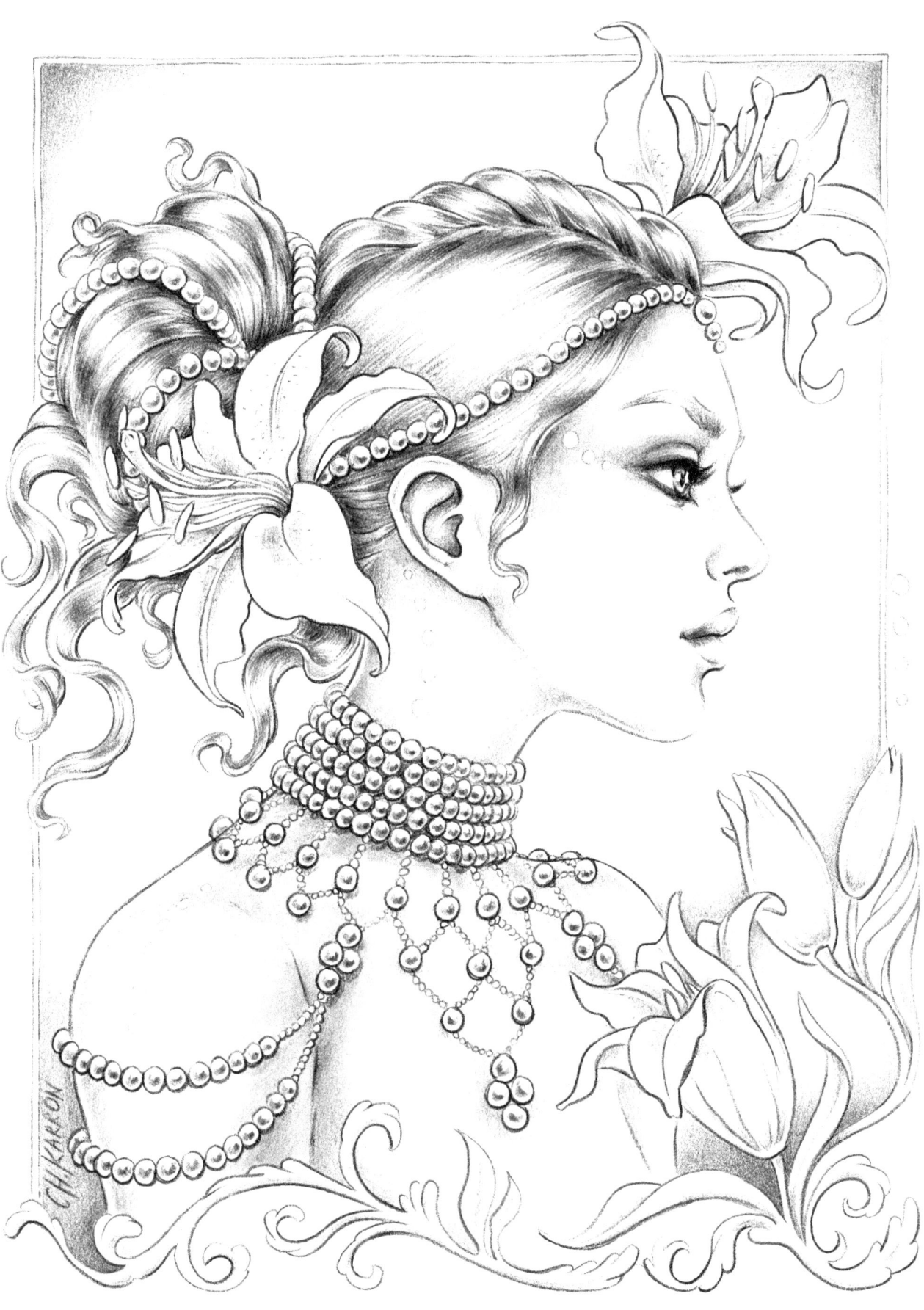

Fairy and Fantasy (c) Christine Karron — Lilies and Pearls

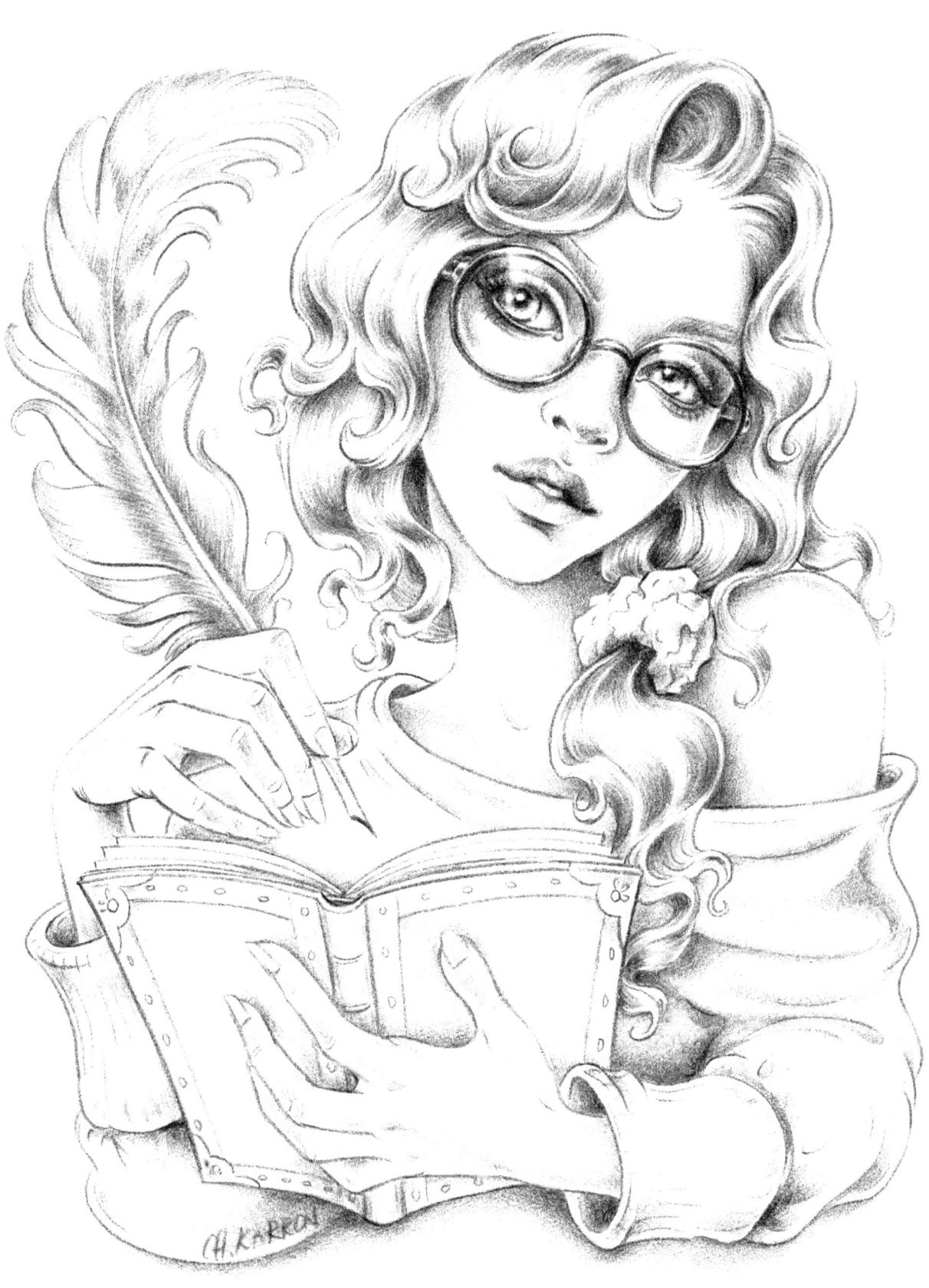

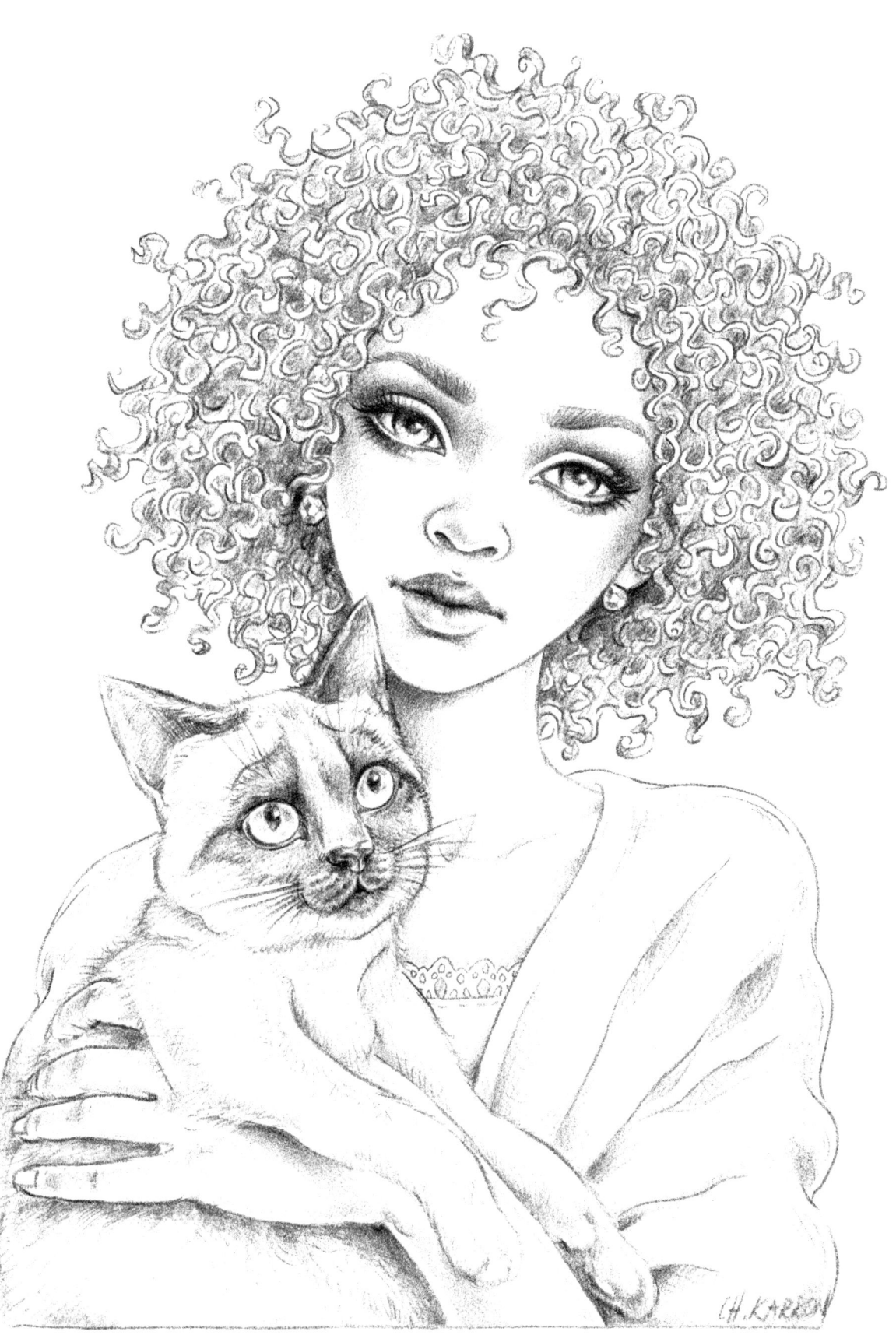

Fairy and Fantasy (c) Christine Karron　　　　　　　　　　Kitty Cuddles

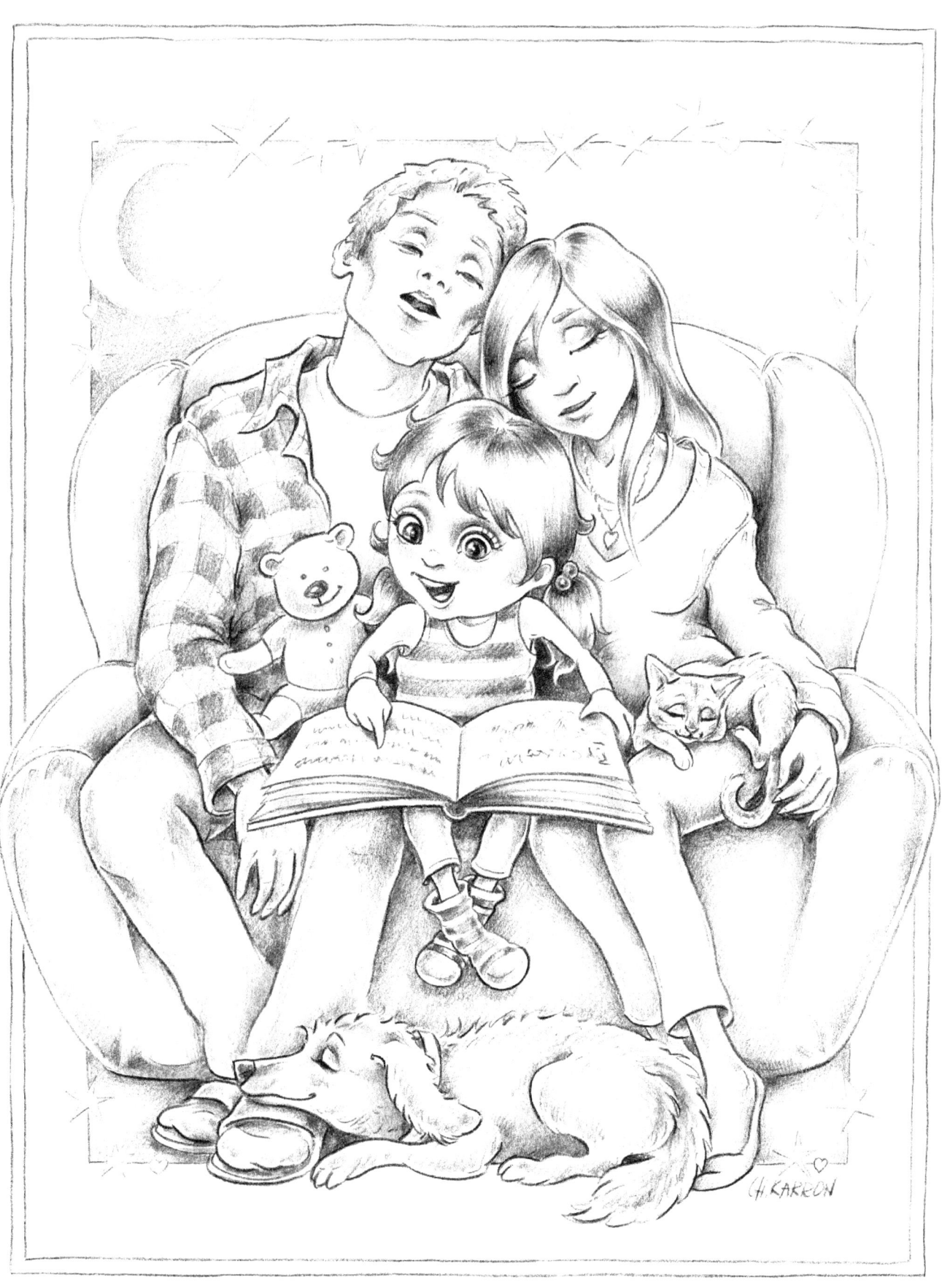

Bedtime Story

Also available:

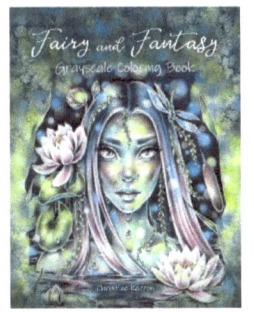 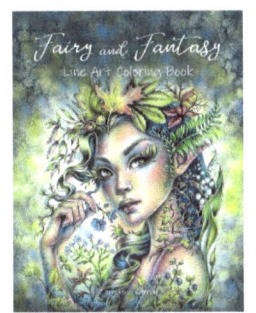 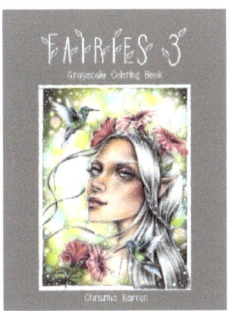 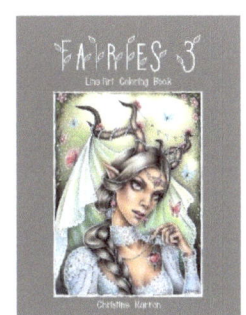

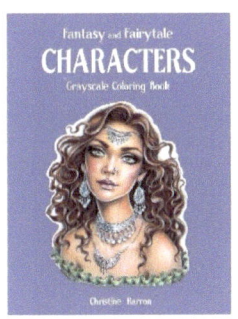 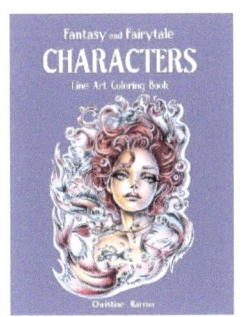 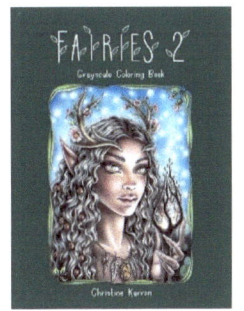 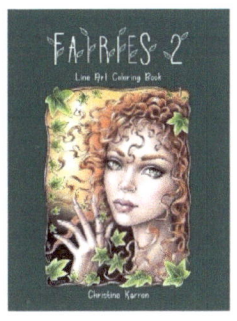

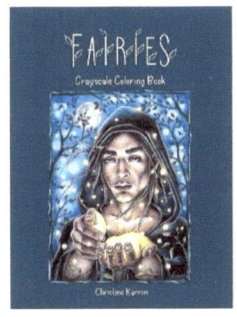 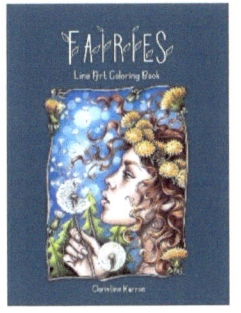 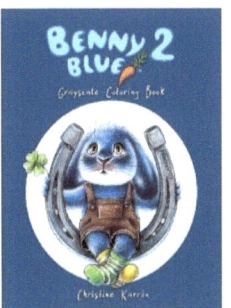 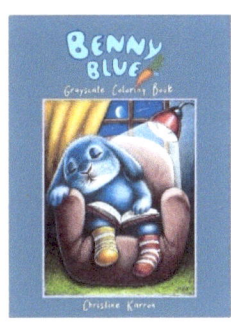

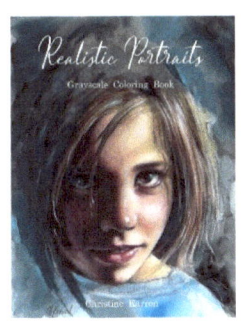 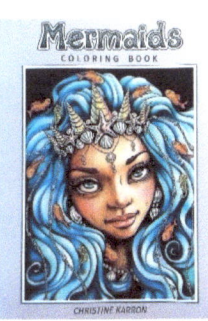 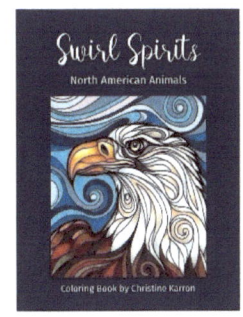

***

Christine Karron is a Canadian artist and illustrator. Drawing and painting has always been her life. With some formal training, self-education and experience, between raising kids and taking care of her family, Christine has been working as a freelance artist for over 20 years.

Working traditionally, Christine loves to create fantasy illustrations and characters with a whimsical, narrative touch. Nature, music and people from her surroundings mostly influence Christine's artwork, as well as precious memories from her childhood when picking flowers and berries in forests so deep like in fairy tales.

Christine's artwork has been sold worldwide, published in books and magazines in Europe as well as in North America. Christine has illustrated six children's books and self-published multiple coloring books.

You can follow Christine Karron on Facebook and Instagram.

Printable digital downloads (in PDF format) of individual coloring pages and sets are available in Christine Karron's Etsy shop.

You are welcome to join Christine Karron
Coloring Collection Fan Group on Facebook.

Visit www.chkarron.com for coloring inspirations,
or watch demo videos on Christine's Youtube channel.

If sharing colored images online please credit the artist Christine Karron.
You can use hashtags #christinekarron and/or #chkarron
Please DO NOT share or post uncolored versions of the images from this book on Facebook, Pinterest or any other sharing sites online.

www.chkarron.com

www.ingramcontent.com/pod-product-compliance
Lightning Source LLC
Chambersburg PA
CBHW051210220526
45473CB00003B/975